Tax Planning For The Statutory Residence Test: 2021/2022

Lee J Hadnum

IMPORTANT LEGAL NOTICES:

WealthProtectionReportTM
TAX GUIDE - "Tax Planning For The Statutory Residence Test: 2021/2022"

Published by:
WealthProtectionReport.co.uk
Email: sales@wealthprotectionreport.co.uk

First Edition: June 2021

Copyright

Copyright © WealthProtectionReport.co.uk All rights reserved.

No part of this publication may be reproduced or transmitted in any form or by any means (electronically or mechanically, including photocopying, recording or storing it in any medium by electronic means) without the prior permission in writing of the copyright owner except in accordance with the provisions of the Copyright, Designs and Patents Act 1988 or under the terms of a licence issued by the Copyright Licensing Agency Ltd, 90 Tottenham Court Road, London, W1P 0LP. All applications for the written permission of the copyright owner to reproduce or transmit any part of this Tax Guide should be sent to the publisher.
Warning: Any unauthorised reproduction or transmission of any part of this Tax Guide may result in criminal prosecution and a civil claim for damages.

Trademarks

The logo "WealthProtectionReportTM" is a trademark of WealthProtectionReport.co.uk. All other logos, trademarks, names and logos in this Tax Guide may be trademarks of their respective owners.

DISCLAIMER

1. Please note that this tax guide is intended as general guidance only for individual readers and does NOT constitute accountancy, tax, legal, investment or other professional advice. WealthProtectionReport and the author accept no responsibility or liability for loss which may arise from reliance on information contained in this tax guide.

2. Please note that tax legislation, the law and practices by government and regulatory authorities (for example, HM Revenue and Customs) are constantly changing and the information contained in this tax guide is only correct as at the date of publication. We therefore recommend that for accountancy, tax, investment or other professional advice, you consult a suitably qualified accountant, tax specialist, independent financial adviser, or other professional adviser. Please also note that your personal circumstances may vary from the general examples given in this tax guide and your professional adviser will be able to give specific advice based on your personal circumstances.

3. This tax guide covers UK taxation mainly and any references to 'tax' or 'taxation' in this tax guide, unless the contrary is expressly stated, are to UK taxation only. Please note that references to the 'UK' do not include the Channel Islands or the Isle of Man. Addressing all foreign tax implications is beyond the scope of this tax guide.

4. Whilst in an effort to be helpful, this tax guide may refer to general guidance on matters other than UK taxation, WealthProtectionReport and the author are not experts in these matters and do not accept any responsibility or liability for loss which may arise from reliance on such information contained in this tax guide.

CONTENTS

1 Introduction

2 How the new Statutory Residence Test applies

3 Reducing Your UK Ties for the Statutory Residence Test

4 How to Avoid Timing Traps

5 Exceptional Days

6 The dangers of the "deemed days" rule with the Statutory Residence Test

7 The Transitional Rules

8 Tax residence for a fiscal nomad

9 Why your spouses residence can have a big impact on your tax residence

10 Using a UK double tax treaty to work in the UK free of UK income tax

Tax Planning For The Statutory Residence Test: 2014/2015

ABOUT THE AUTHOR

Lee Hadnum LLB ACA CTA is a UK tax specialist. He is a Chartered Accountant and Chartered Tax Adviser and is the Editor of the popular tax planning website www.wealthprotectionreport.co.uk

Email Lee directly at:

Lee@wealthprotectionreport.co.uk with tax planning questions.

Members of www.wealthprotectionreport.co.uk can access thousands of articles and free tax planning books.

Lee is also the author of a number of best selling tax planning books including:

Tax Planning Techniques Of The Rich & Famous - Essential reading for anyone who wants to use the same tax planning techniques as the most successful Entrepreneurs, large corporations and celebrities

The Worlds Best Tax Havens 2021/2022 – 220 page book looking at the worlds best offshore jurisdictions in detail

Non Resident & Offshore Tax Planning– Offshore tax planning for UK residents or anyone looking to purchase UK property or trade in the UK. A comprehensive guide.

Tax Planning With Offshore Companies & Trusts: The A-Z Guide - Detailed analysis of when and how you can use offshore companies and trusts to reduce your UK taxes

Tax Planning For Company Owners – How company owners can reduce income tax, corporation tax and NICs

Buy To Let Tax Planning – How property investors can reduce income tax, CGT and inheritance tax

Asset Protection Handbook – Looks at strategies to ringfence your assets in today's increasing litigious climate

Working Overseas Guide – Comprehensive analysis of how you can save tax when working overseas

Double Tax Treaty Planning – How you can use double tax treaties to reduce UK taxes

1. INTRODUCTION

As from April 2013 there is a new way of assessing an individuals residence status.

The new Statutory Residence Test provides a comprehensive method of clearly establishing when an individual will (and won't) be UK resident.

Before April 2013 determining your residence status was mainly dependent on applying HMRC practice and various court decisions to your own circumstances. The position after April 2013 is therefore much more clear cut in many cases.

Nevertheless, the Statutory Residence rules are not necessarily straightforward to apply. In this guide we provide some detailed guidance as to how the new rules work and some of the main tax planning areas that you should consider.

2. HOW THE STATUTORY RESIDENCE TEST APPLIES

In the March 2011 Budget it was announced that HMRC would be consulting on a new statutory residence test ("SRT"). This was initially supposed to be implemented from 6th April 2012. However, it was postponed to allow more time for consultation.

It now applies from April 2013.

Given that the UK residency rules are extremely vague, the introduction of a more concrete test for UK residence, laid down in legislation, makes life much easier for anyone wanting to leave the UK.

How Does The Statutory Residence Test Work?

The test brings a range of "key" factors into account when assessing residence. Rather than considering a lot of vague and uncertain factors, you can determine your residence by looking at the factors laid out in the legislation.

Legislation focuses on the key UK ties such as having UK accommodation, UK family or UK employment. Other less important ties such as UK clubs, UK burial plot ownership, and UK bank accounts are not included in the new test.

Therefore, in most cases you will only need to consider the specific factors laid out in the legislation.

There is still the odd subjective element to the new rules. For instance having a UK home will make you automatically UK resident in many cases. However "home" isn't accurately defined and you need to look at whether, on the facts, a UK property is your home.

There is also a system of recognising that to establish non

residence, there can be more ties with the UK if there are fewer visits. They use a scale which takes account of different UK ties according to the length of UK visits and whether you are a "leaver" or an "arriver".

The test has been designed so that it is harder to become non-resident when leaving the UK after a period of residence than it is to become resident when an individual comes to the UK.

Once an individual has become resident and built up connections with the UK, they should be required to scale back their ties to the UK significantly, spend far less time here, or a combination of the two before they can relinquish residence.

This is consistent with the principle, reflected in case law, that residence should have an adhesive nature.

How the New Statutory Residence Test Operates

There are 3 main classifications:

- People who will always be non-resident
- People who will always be UK resident
- Others who may be UK resident or may be non-resident depending on their UK visits and ties.

People who are always non-resident

For UK residents leaving the UK, this will apply to anyone leaving the UK to work under a full-time contract overseas.

They won't need to sever UK ties and they'll be non-resident from the date of departure. This applies providing UK visits are fewer than 91 days in the tax year and no more than 30 days are spent working in the UK in the tax year (this is defined as spending more than 3 hours per day working in the UK).

It's also important that there are no significant breaks (31 continuous days or more) from the overseas 'work'.

You need to determine whether the person works an average of 35 hours per week abroad over the course of the tax year.

As well as anyone meeting the above conditions, it will also apply to anyone who is:

- Not resident in the UK in all of the previous three tax years and they are present in the UK for fewer than 46 days in the current tax year; or
- Resident in the UK in one or more of the previous three tax years and they are present in the UK for fewer than 16 days in the current tax year.

So, if you've been UK resident for the last few years unless you can arrange your return visits to be less than 16 days for the next 3 years you'll only qualify for automatic non-residence if you go to work overseas.

Nevertheless, this is a great opportunity for someone leaving the UK.

You can leave the UK and spend up to 16 days in the UK for the first 3 years and thereafter up to 46 days irrespective of the number of ties you have in the UK. It would not matter if you had UK family or accommodation. So long as you keep your visits to within these limits you would be non-UK resident.

People definitely UK resident

If the above does not apply then you will definitely be UK resident if:

- You are present in the UK for 183 days or more in a tax year; or
- You have only one home and that home is in the UK (or you have two or more homes and all of these are in the UK); or
- You carry out full-time work in the UK

This will effectively catch anyone who in reality has their home or job in the UK but looks to argue that they are non-resident.

When do you carry our full time work in the UK?

HMRC classes you as UK resident if you work full time in the UK for 365 days or more with no significant break from UK work.

In order to be caught by this rule (and therefore be automatically UK resident) you need to spend more than 75% of the total number of days in the tax year when you do more than three hours work, working in the UK.

The reference to "significant break" is interesting. HMRC state that you will have a significant break from UK work if at least 31 days go by and not one of those days is a day on which you:

- work for more than three hours, or
- would have worked for more than three hours, but you do not do so because you are on annual leave, sick leave or parenting leave.

Having an Overseas Home

Having an overseas home will be an important issue. HMRC have provided additional details on when having a UK home will make you UK resident if you also have an overseas home.

You will be UK resident where:

- you have a home in the UK for a period of more than 90 days

- you are present in that UK home on at least 30 separate days (individual or consecutive days) during the tax year, and

- while you have that UK home, there is a period of 91 consecutive days, some or all of which falls within the tax year in question, when you have no home overseas, or have one or more homes overseas in none of which you are present for more than 30 (not necessarily consecutive) days during the tax year.

Therefore, you need to assess whether there is a period of 91 consecutive days, falling partly within the tax year when you have a home in the UK and no home overseas (or a home which is occupied for 30 days or less in the tax year). You also need to be present in your UK home on at least 30 days during the tax year.

If you meet all these conditions you would be UK resident.

If you have more than one home in the UK, you should consider each of those homes separately to see if you meet the test. You need only meet this test in relation to one of your homes.

If you have a UK home and an overseas home and want to avoid being UK resident by virtue of this condition one option could be to:

- Make sure that your overseas home is available for at least 91 days

- Ensure that you spend at least 30 days each tax year in your overseas home.

The rules relating to this "home" connection are complex, and anyone who thinks this could apply to them should consider the dates of their UK return visits and occupation of overseas properties very carefully.

What if I have more than one overseas home?

Based on the notes issued by HMRC, you would consider each home separately to assess whether it meets the 30-day requirement. It should apply irrespective of where the property is located.

People who could be UK resident or non-resident

This will apply to most people leaving the UK and takes account of the different ties that people can have to the UK and overseas.

It reflects the principle that the more time someone spends in the UK, the fewer connections they have with the UK if they want to be non-resident.

It also incorporates the principle that residence status should adhere more to those who are already resident than to those who are not currently resident.

The following five connection factors are relevant to an individual's residence status, but only when linked to the amount of time the person spends in the UK:

- Family - the individual's spouse, civil partner, common law equivalent (provided the individual is not separated from them) or minor children are resident in the UK

- Accommodation - the individual has accessible accommodation in the UK and makes use of it during the tax year (subject to exclusions for some types of accommodation)

- Substantive work in the UK - the individual does substantive work in the UK (but does not work in the UK full-time)

- UK presence in previous years - the individual spent 90 days or more in the UK in either of the previous two tax years

- More time in the UK than in other countries - the individual spends more days in the UK in the tax year than in any other single country.

These connection factors would be combined with days spent in the UK into a "scale" to determine whether the individual is resident or not.

Leavers

When someone is leaving the UK and was resident in one or more of the three tax years immediately preceding the tax year of departure, the scale of factors to take into account where he or she spends:

- fewer than 16 days in the UK, he or she is always non-resident

- 16 to 45 days in the UK, he or she is resident only if four or more factors apply

- 46 to 90 days in the UK, he or she is resident only if three or more factors apply

- 91 to 120 days in the UK, he or she is resident only if two or more factors apply

- 121 to 182 days in the UK, he or she is resident only if one or more factors apply

- 183 days or more in the UK, he or she is always resident.

If you want to remain non-resident your limits are:

- 0 connection factors – up to 182 days
- 1 connection factor – up to 120 days
- 2 connection factors – up to 90 days
- 3 connection factors – up to 45 days
- 4 connection factors – up to 15 days

Arrivers

In the case of someone arriving in the UK and who has not been UK resident during the previous three tax years, the scale of factors is more attractive.

Where he or she spends:

- fewer than 46 days in the UK, he or she is always non-resident

- 46 to 90 days in the UK, he or she is resident only if four factors apply

- 91 to 120 days in the UK, he or she is resident only if three or more factors apply

- 121 to 182 days in the UK, he or she is resident only if two or more factors apply

- 183 days or more in the UK, he or she is always resident

This is a novel system for recognising ties. For most people who are genuinely leaving the UK, it would be welcomed.

The main thrust of the Statutory Residence Test is to combat people looking to artificially avoid being UK resident whilst retaining strong UK links.

Most people who leave the UK look to reduce their UK visits. This would reduce their possible UK ties to just 1 or 2 from the above list. This is likely to be highly satisfactory and ensure that UK available accommodation could be retained in certain cases.

Example
Johnny is a long-term UK resident. He decides to leave the UK permanently at a time when the statutory residence test is in operation (in the proposed form discussed above).

Because Johnny has been UK resident throughout each of the previous three tax years, he will not automatically be non-UK resident when he leaves the UK, unless he is leaving under a full-time contract of employment or spends fewer than 16 days in the UK during the current tax year. We will assume that neither of these circumstances applies.

Johnny would not automatically be UK resident either, unless he spent more than 183 days in the UK during the tax year, had his only home(s) in the UK or was working in the UK. Again, we'll assume that these circumstances do not apply in Johnny's case.

Whether he is UK resident or not will depend on the type of connections he has to the UK and the number of days he spends in the UK.

Having UK available accommodation is just one factor. Providing he clearly establishes a home overseas, he could retain his UK accommodation, as long as he restricts his other UK connecting factors and his UK visits.

Therefore, if we assume his wife and minor child go overseas with him and he is not planning on carrying out any work in the UK, he would at most have two connecting factors, providing he spends more time in his new overseas country of residence than the UK. This means he could visit the UK for up to 90 days during the tax year without being classed as UK resident.

Anti Avoidance Rule

Residence in a Nutshell

As you can see, residence issues can be fairly complex. As a summary:

- An individual who is UK resident and domiciled will be liable to UK tax on his/her worldwide income and gains.

- An individual who is UK resident but not UK domiciled can claim to be liable to UK tax on overseas income/gains only when the income/proceeds are remitted to the UK, subject to various requirements. This is known as the remittance basis.

- An individual who is non-resident will be liable to UK income tax on UK source income but will be exempt from UK capital gains tax on all assets (whether situated in the UK or overseas), except for assets used in a UK trade or UK immovable property.

Example 1

John, who is UK domiciled, has purchased a villa in Spain and intends to spend as much time there as possible.

He stays 10 months in the villa and, in order to supplement his income, rents out his property in the UK through a letting agent on a long lease and obtains a small part-time job in a Spanish vineyard, tasting local wines. He has sold all of his other UK investments. When he is not in the villa makes short trips to the UK to visit friends and spends the rest of his time travelling.

He would need to spend less than 16 days in the UK to be automatically non-resident, given he has not gone overseas under a full-time contract of employment. We'll assume he doesn't meet this requirement.

He should not be automatically UK resident and therefore it would be a case of looking at his UK ties. He could be classed as having UK accommodation (due to his UK trips) but even assuming this was the case, he should have just two ties so long as he doesn't have UK family.

From a UK tax perspective, he will be regarded as non-UK resident as he could visit for up to 90 days with two UK ties (but in fact spends much less than this). Therefore:

- His UK source income (in other words, rental income) will be subject to UK income tax.
- His overseas income (his income from his part-time job in Spain) will not be subject to UK taxation.

3. REDUCING YOUR UK TIES FOR THE STATUTORY RESIDENCE TEST

The above shows how important it can be to reduce your UK ties.

If you are leaving the UK for instance, reducing your UK ties from 3 to 2 means that you can spend around an extra month and a half in the UK in the tax year without being classed as UK resident.

By paying careful attention to how the various ties are defined, there are opportunities to reduce your UK ties and maximise your UK visits.

UK Accommodation Tie

Firstly, this is completely different to the "UK Home" condition that can make you automatically UK resident.

A UK home is much narrower in scope and will affect far less people. Accommodation can be pretty much anything (house, caravan, houseboat and other property) and does not even need to be owned by you.

You are classed as having a UK accommodation tie if there is any accommodation that is available for your use while you are in the UK.

It must be available to you for a continuous period of at least 91 days during the tax year and you must use it for at least one night during that tax year.

So if you had accommodation available in the UK but never stayed there during a specific tax year you wouldn't have a UK accommodation tie.

In some circumstances (depending on the number of days you are returning for) you may be better off staying somewhere in the UK that isn't classed as an accommodation.

Staying in other people's property

Just because you don't own a UK property, this does not mean that you can't be classed as having UK accommodation.

However, who owns the property you stay in can have a big impact on you:

- If you stay at the home of a "close relative", the property will be classed as an accommodation tie if you spend at least 16 nights there in any one tax year and it is available to you for a continuous period of at least 91 days.

- A "close relative" is defined as a parent, grandparent, brother, sister and child or grandchild aged 18 or over (whether or not they are blood relatives or related by marriage or civil partnership). Child includes any adopted children.

- By contrast, if you stay in any other property owned by anyone else, this action is classed as an accommodation tie if you spend at least 1 night there. This also applies to UK accommodation held by a spouse, partner or minor children.

This means that wherever possible it makes sense to stay with "Close Relatives" as defined above if your total visits will be less than 16 days in the tax year.

Types of accommodation that are excluded

HMRC have listed a few types of accommodation that won't give rise to a UK accommodation tie:

- Accommodation owned by an individual but wholly let out commercially would not be considered as available to live in unless they retained the right to use the property or part of the property.

- Accommodation that is available to an individual but in which they have not spent at least one night in the tax year will not be an accommodation tie.

- Short stays at hotels and guesthouses will not usually be considered to be an accommodation tie. However, if an individual books a room in the same hotel or guesthouse (and does not cancel those bookings) for at least 91 days continuously in a tax year it will be an accommodation tie.

UK Family

Having UK family is classed as a tie to the UK.

UK family is just one of the "Sufficient Ties" tests and is not on its own enough to make an individual UK resident.

As long as an emigrant kept UK ties to two, they could still visit for up to 90 days per tax year and remain non-resident.

For instance, if they had a UK wife and children that they actually visited and owned or rented UK accommodation (assuming of course they were not UK resident in either of the previous two tax years).

What is a family tie?

HMRC class you as having a family tie if any of the following people are UK resident:

- your husband, wife or civil partner (unless you are separated) your partner, if you are living together as husband and wife or as civil partners
- your child, if under 18-years-old, unless:

✓ you see your child in person, in the UK on a total of 60 days or fewer in the tax year concerned, or

✓ if your child turns 18 during that tax year, you see your child in person, in the UK on a total of 60 days or fewer in the part of the tax year before their 18th birthday.

Children in education in the UK are not included, providing they spend fewer than 21 days in the UK outside term-time.

Any day or part of a day that you meet your child in person, in the UK is included in this 60 day count.

This is a difficult definition to sidestep – particularly where your partner is living in the UK, and you are not separated.

If just your child was in the UK (for instance you were separated from your UK partner), you could avoid having a UK family tie by avoiding UK visits of more than 60 days. Your child could visit you overseas without this having any impact on the family ties condition.

UK presence in previous years

If you spend 90 days or more in the UK in either of the previous two tax years, this is classed as an additional UK tie ("UK Presence Tie").

This is an important point to bear in mind.

These connection factors directly link into how long an individual can spend in the UK in a tax year before they are classed as UK resident.

So, for example, an individual will be non-UK resident if they spend 90 to 119 days in the UK in a tax year provided that they are:

- Arrivers with no more than 2 connection factors
  or
- Leavers with no more than 1 connection factor

Watch Out

Be aware that if an individual spends more than 90 days in the UK in a tax year, this will in itself be a connection factor for the following two tax years.

This adds an extra factor to the number of connection factors the individual already had, possibly taking him or her over a threshold and making them UK resident.

Example

Jack is a new Arriver in 2021/22. He has a UK resident wife and also accommodation in the UK (i.e. 2 connection factors). He spends 95 days in the UK in 2021/22 and 45 days in the UK in 2022/23.

He will not be resident in those tax years if he does not work in the UK or have his home in the UK. If Jack then spends 95 days in the UK in 2023/24, he will become UK resident since he will then have 3 connection factors (family, accommodation and more than 90 days spent in the UK in one of the previous two tax years).

In 2024/25 Jack will no longer be an Arriver, because he was resident in 2023/24. This means he now has to apply the more stringent tests for Leavers. As a Leaver with 3 connection factors he will not be able to spend more than 45 days in the UK if he wishes to lose his UK residence.

This example about Jack demonstrates that individuals who wish to remain non-UK resident should still spend fewer than 90 days per tax year in the UK, unless they can reduce their other connection factors/UK ties to a number that will preserve their non-resident status.

Substantive work in the UK

You have a Work Tie to the UK if you do substantive work in the UK (but do not work in the UK full-time). If you did work in the UK full-time you'd be likely to be classed as automatically UK resident.

You are classed as having substantive work in the UK if you do more than three hours work a day in the UK for a total of at least 40 days in that year.

This also includes self-employed individuals.

Work is defined very widely: unless you are undertaking a voluntary post and have no employment contract/contract of service, most of your activities related to your profession or UK employment activity will be classed as work for this purpose.

Avoid having a UK "Home"

As we've seen above, broadly speaking provided you are not treated as automatically overseas resident, you will be UK resident if you have a home in the UK for more than 90 days; are present on at least 30 separate days during the tax year and, whilst you have that home, there is at least one period of 91 consecutive days (some or all of which falls within the tax year in question) when you either have no home overseas or none in which you are present for more than 30 days.

Therefore, deciding what constitutes a home and, if you have more than one, monitoring how much time you spend at each, will be of vital importance.

Unfortunately the Revenue have acknowledged that defining "a home" exhaustively is too difficult. They assert that the vast majority of taxpayers will know whether and where they have a home and so they have provided only limited statutory definitions and guidance!

For those who do instinctively know where their home is, the legislation may muddy the waters a little.

A home can be any part of a building, vehicle, vessel or structure with the requisite degree of permanence (e.g. a mobile home, houseboat) and you do not necessarily have to own any interest in it (e.g. living at a parents house may count).

In addition a property can still be your home even if you do not continually live there (particularly if your spouse or children remain in the property) or if it is temporarily unavailable (e.g. due to a fire or building works).

Somewhere used periodically as a holiday home or a temporary retreat is not a home.

However, HMRC give an example in their guidance of the way in which a property can change from a holiday home to a home, which demonstrates some of the conceptual difficulties:

A woman lives and works in the UK but owns an apartment in Spain which she rents out apart from two to three weeks a year when she takes her holiday there. The Spanish property is not her home. However, she then decides to live in the Spanish apartment throughout the British winter, from October to March. Her use of the property has changed from being somewhere she used for an occasional short break to somewhere she uses as a home for part of the year.

This example may be quite clear cut, but what if she had decided to spend a shorter period there each winter (say two months)? Does this indicate that the Spanish property is a home she is living in or is it just a holiday home she is using for a longer period?

To reach a conclusion you would need to consider all relevant circumstances.

Once you have worked out where your homes are, you then need to consider how much time you spend in each and over what period, which again may result in some surprising conclusions.

A further Revenue example demonstrates the potential difficulties:

A man has lived in Australia all his life. In June 2020 he takes a holiday in London and likes it so much he decides to emigrate to the UK. He spends the next few months preparing for the move. He sells his Australian house (his only home) on 10 January 2022 and arrives in the UK on 25 January 2022. He finds a flat in London and moves in on 1 February 2022.

The London flat is now his only home and he lives there for a year. During tax year 2021-22 he is present in his Australian home on 250 days, and he is present in his London flat on 55 days.

There is a period of 91 consecutive days falling partly within tax year 2021-22 (the period starting on 1 February 2022) when he has a home in the UK and no home overseas. During tax year 2021-22 he is present in that UK home on at least 30 days. He does not meet the overseas residence test and is therefore automatically UK resident.

This is surprising, as he has only had a home in the UK for a couple of months in 2021-22 and for the majority of the year, his only home was in Australia.

If you have a home in the UK you will have to pay close attention to these new rules, particularly where you spend your time outside the UK in a number of different countries.

Country tie

This tie applies to leavers only and applies where an individual spends more days in the UK than any other single country in the tax year.

4. HOW TO AVOID TIMING TRAPS

The decision as to whether you are resident needs to be made for an entire tax year. In other words, you are not normally resident for part of a tax year.

Example 1

Keith is present in the UK from 6th April 2021 to 7th October 2021 (185 days). He would be resident in the UK for the entire 2021/22 tax year.

In practice, an exception used to be made to this rule where a person leaves the UK to take up a 'permanent' residence elsewhere. Such a person is regarded as resident in the UK from 6th April to the date of his departure. In other words, rather than being regarded as UK resident for the whole of the tax year, the individual will be regarded as non-resident for the period that he is overseas.

This treatment is known as 'split year' treatment and was allowed by way of a Revenue and Customs concession. In fact, its use is widespread - particularly for income tax purposes. There are significant restrictions on its use for capital gains tax purposes.

In the case of someone leaving the UK, it means that they are only subject to UK income tax on foreign income up to the point they leave the UK. After they leave the UK, they are then not subject to UK income tax.

The statutory residence test

A tax year will only be split into periods of residence and non-residence in a specific number of defined cases.

These are:

- You become resident in the UK if you start to have a home in the UK;
- You become resident by starting full-time employment in the UK or by going to live in the UK;
- You lose UK residence by establishing your only home in a country outside the UK;
- You lose UK residence by virtue of working full-time abroad or by returning to the UK after you cease working abroad (or your partner does).

They also include a useful table that reduces the 90 day visit limit in the tax year that you leave, dependent on the month that you leave the UK (i.e. if you left in May you could visit for 82 days, compared to just 7 if you left in March).

This will therefore significantly reduce the occasions when the split year basis will apply. HMRC have specifically stated that the various other occasions when you lose UK residence (the sufficient ties factors such as having UK family) won't be taken into account when considering the split year basis.

As stated earlier, this can make ceasing to have a UK home and establishing your only home overseas very attractive in the tax year that you leave the UK.

Establishing Your Main Home Overseas

If you want to claim the split year basis and make your main home overseas you need to make sure that within six months of departure your normal home is overseas.

You can also spend up to 16 days in the UK in the year of departure.

In addition:

- you must have been resident in the previous tax year (this includes where the previous year was a split year);
- must cease to have a UK home in the tax year
- must be non-resident in the following year.

From the point you cease to have a home in the UK, you must spend fewer than 16 days in the UK and either:

✓ become tax resident in another country within 6 months; or
✓ be present in another country at the end of each day for 6 months; or
✓ have your only home or all your homes if you have more than one, in another country.

It's not strictly necessary to establish your home overseas. Rather you need to cease to have a UK home and then either establish tax residence overseas, be present in another country for 6 months or establish an overseas home.

In most cases the above will entail establishing your home overseas in any case.

It's also worth noting that the above, combined with the rest of the provisions make it clear that in order to lose UK tax residence it is not necessary to establish tax residence overseas. You could also still claim the split year basis even without tax residence overseas.

The above may make it more difficult for transient individuals such as fiscal nomads to claim the split year basis in the year of departure.

Starting to have a home in the UK

One of the main ways you can take advantage of the split year basis in the year of your arrival back to the UK is to start to have a home in the UK.

The rules state that you will qualify for split year treatment where:

- you were non-resident for the previous tax year and are UK resident for the following tax year (and that year is not a split year) and
- at a point during the year you they have a home located in the UK for the first time and this remains the case for the rest of the year and the whole of the next tax year.

In addition, before that point in the year you must not have sufficient UK ties to make you UK resident for that part of the year considered in isolation.

This last point means that you would need to consider the various connecting factors under the statutory residence test (UK accommodation, Family ties, Work ties etc) and ascertain whether you would be classed as resident under the rules for the part of the tax year before you return to the UK.

There is a special table with amended days that varies according to your date of arrival into the UK.

5. EXCEPTIONAL DAYS

Days that are regarded as "exceptional" are excluded when considering the various tests in the Statutory Residence Test.

There is however a limit of 60 exceptional days per tax year. If you spend more than 60 days in the UK and these all arise from exceptional circumstances only 60 days will be disregarded. The remainder will count as days in the UK for the various residence tests.

So what are exceptional circumstances?

The definition needs to be deliberately vague as by definition they are difficult to foresee and could be anything from national or local emergencies to plane strikes to sudden illness.

HMRC defines exceptional circumstances as days spent in the UK if the individual's presence in the UK is due to exceptional circumstances beyond their control.

It's therefore essentially something that keeps them in the UK and is:
- outside of their control
  - something over which they effectively have no choice
  - something which cannot reasonably have been foreseen

Types of scenarios where HMRC accept there are exceptional circumstances include:
- local or national emergencies, such as civil unrest or natural disasters,
- the outbreak of war
- sudden serious or life threatening illness or injury
- plane delays which require you to remain in the UK until the next available flight

- serious illness or injury of a loved one whilst in the UK

What aren't exceptional circumstances?

Events such as birth, marriage, divorce and death are not usually regarded as exceptional circumstances.

In addition choosing to come to the UK for medical treatment or to receive elective medical services such as dentistry, cosmetic surgery or therapies also won't qualify as exceptional circumstances.

Covid-19

The Government introduced new guidance on what can be classed as an exceptional day due to having to remain in the UK due to the Covid-19 restrictions.

This includes where a taxpayer is:

- Quarantined or advised by a health professional to self-isolate in the UK as a result of the virus;
- Advised by official Government advice not to travel from the UK as a result of the virus;
- Unable to leave the UK due to the closure of international borders; or
- Asked by an employer to return to the UK temporarily as a result of the virus.

6. THE DANGERS OF THE "DEEMED DAYS" RULE WITH THE STATUTORY RESIDENCE TEST

The day tests under the "Sufficient Ties" test in particular can be favourable to anyone leaving the UK.

By carefully limiting UK ties emigrants can still spend significant periods in the UK without being classed as UK resident.

In earlier guidance on the Statutory Residence Test, HMRC made it clear they were looking at some form of restriction where an individual makes a lot of separate visits to the UK.

This was formed into the "Deemed Days" provisions.

You are only classed as spending a day in the UK if you are in the UK at midnight. For someone arriving on Friday and leaving on Monday, they would have Friday, Saturday and Sunday as days spent in the UK.

Where the deeming rule applies, the test can count days that you are not in the UK at midnight as days spent in the UK.

In practice the deeming rule will applies to someone who makes numerous return visits back to the UK.

When will the deeming rule apply?

The deeming rule applies where you:

- have at least three UK ties for the tax year, and

- have been present in the UK on more than 30 days in the tax year, without being present at the end of that day ('qualifying days'), and

- have been UK resident in one or more of the preceding three tax years.

If you meet these conditions, only the first 30 qualifying days are excluded. All other days above 30 are classed as days spent in the UK for the UK residence tests.

Key points

A qualifying day is effectively a day that you leave the UK. The aim of the deeming rule is to catch people who make frequent short visits back to the UK.

Based on the standard residence tests they may well be non-resident due to having a low number of days in the UK, but when you class the days of departure as deeming days they may well be UK resident.

For most people though, 30 qualifying days should be more than sufficient, and it will only be extremely frequent UK visitors who will need to consider this rule. Even then once they have established non residence for 3 years it won't be immediately relevant. You also need to have 3 UK ties under the Sufficient Ties test before the deeming rule applies.

If you have 2 UK ties and need to decide whether or not you have spent more than 90 days in the UK in either or both of the previous two tax years (which would make your 3rd UK tie), you exclude the deeming rule and only count days you were actually in the UK at midnight.

8. TAX RESIDENCE FOR A FISCAL NOMAD -

The basic principle behind the idea of becoming a fiscal nomad is to exploit the residency rules in a number of countries so that you're not caught by any one country's tax net. Most people will do this by either travelling continuously or basing themselves in a handful of countries and only spending a few months in each. Providing care is taken as to the length of stay you could simply be treated as a tourist in each country and be exempted from any requirement to pay income tax.

In practice of course. travelling continuously can usually only be maintained for a few years due to the other burdens of being so nomadic, and it is the second option of splitting your time between a few well chosen countries that is most popular.

However, in terms of UK tax can you actually avoid being UK resident if you leave the UK and don't establish tax residence overseas?

The statutory residence test provides specific statutory rules that where followed will provide certainty as to residence status.

Finance Act 2013 contains the relevant provisions.

It starts by stating:

"The basic rule

3 An individual ("P") is resident in the UK for a tax year ("year X") if-

*(a) the automatic residence test is met for that year,
or (b) the sufficient ties test is met for that year.*

4 If neither of those tests is met for that year, P is not resident in the UK for that year."

It then states

"...5 The automatic residence test is met for year X if P meets-

(a) at least one of the automatic UK tests, and
(b) none of the automatic overseas tests..."

Therefore if you meet an "automatic overseas test" you shouldn't be UK resident.

Looking at the "automatic overseas test" it states:

"11 There are 5 automatic overseas tests.

12 The first automatic overseas test is that-

(a) P was resident in the UK for one or more of the 3 tax years preceding year X,

(b) the number of days in year X that P spends in the UK is less than 16, and

(c) P does not die in year X.

13 The second automatic overseas test is that-

(a) P was resident in the UK for none of the 3 tax years preceding year X, and

(b) the number of days that P spends in the UK in year X is less than 46..."

Therefore for most UK residents leaving the UK they should be able to establish non residence if they spend less than 46 days in the UK in a tax year. There is no mention of having to establish tax residence overseas.

When does the legislation require tax residence overseas?

Looking through the legislation there is just one occasion where foreign tax residence is taken into account. This applies when an individual is looking to establish the split year basis when they leave the UK. There are 5 different occasions where the split year basis can be claimed. Number 3 applies where an individual ceases to have a home in the UK.

The legislation states:

"...Case 3: ceasing to have a home in the UK

46 (1) The circumstances of a case fall within Case 3 if they are as described in sub-paragraphs (2) to (6).

(2) The taxpayer was resident in the UK for the previous tax year (whether or not it was a split year).

(3) At the start of the relevant year the taxpayer had one or more homes in the UK but-

(a) there comes a day in the relevant year when P ceases to have any home in the UK, and

(b) from then on, P has no home in the UK for the rest of that year.

(4) In the part of the relevant year beginning with the day mentioned in sub-paragraph (3)(a), the taxpayer spends fewer than 16 days in the UK.

(5) The taxpayer is not resident in the UK for the next tax year.

(6) At the end of the period of 6 months beginning with the day mentioned in sub-paragraph (3)(a), the taxpayer has a sufficient link with a country overseas.

(7)The taxpayer has a "sufficient link" with a country overseas if and only if-

(a)the taxpayer is considered for tax purposes to be a resident of that country in accordance with its domestic laws, or

(b)the taxpayer has been present in that country (in person) at the end of each day of the 6-month period mentioned in sub-paragraph (6), or

(c)the taxpayer's only home is in that country or, if the taxpayer has more than one home, they are all in that country..."

Therefore, tax residence overseas can be taken into account for the split year basis.

9. Why your spouse's residence can have a big impact on your tax residence

When looking at automatic UK residence under the statutory residence test, the first UK tie is whether you have a spouse who is resident in the UK for the year.

That creates its own difficulties because you have to investigate carefully the circumstances of your spouse to make sure that you do not inadvertently have an extra UK tie.

Actually, it does not have to be a spouse; it can be someone with whom you are living as husband and wife -- which is thought to mean that you live together not as husband and wife but in a way which looks like husband and wife.

If you have a place to live in the UK and spent more than 90 days here last year, you will have 2 UK ties. As an arriver, you would be able to spend 120 days in the UK during the tax year without becoming resident.

However, it would be a bit of a problem if you were to discover that your spouse was UK resident thereby giving you an additional UK Tie and reducing your allowable days to only 90.

Clearly, communication between husbands and wives takes on a whole new dimension.

Let us look at a straightforward example. You made a capital gain on a share disposal in 2021/22. You were not resident because you had insufficient UK days or ties to become UK resident and (subject to the temporary non residence rules) the capital gain will potentially be free of tax.

However, if your wife was resident during that year, that would give you an additional UK tie which would cause you to be UK resident and a substantial charge to capital gains tax would arise.

The residence of your wife is therefore crucial. Whether your wife was resident will depend upon her day count and this will depend upon which day count table applied to her for the year -- and that will depend on whether she was an arriver or a leaver, that is to say whether she was resident in the UK for any of the previous 3 years.

Establishing her residence for those earlier years would be quite difficult under the old rules but we can of course make the election under Schedule 45(154) FA 2013 to apply the new rules for this purpose. We therefore need to look at her day count for the years 2018/19 and 2019/20.

Before they were married

However, you might not even have met her by then - let alone married her -- so your liability to UK capital gains tax for 2021/22 could depend upon the number of days that somebody who you did not know in 2018 had spent in the UK during that year. If she had spent more than the relevant number of days in 2018, that could have made her resident for 2018/19 for the purposes of the Statutory Residence Test which would make her a leaver and subject to the less generous day count table causing her to be resident in 2021/22.

You may think that because you tend to spend the same number of days in the UK together, if you were non-resident, so was she. But not if she is an arriver and you are a leaver. You would be subject to different day count tables.

Of course there's no way that her advisers could have told her in 2018 to be careful how many days she spends in the UK because in a few years time she might marry somebody and he might make a capital gain and the number of days she spent in the UK during 2018 could cost him millions of pounds in capital gains tax in January 2023.

Similarly your advisers couldn't have told you that if you meet somebody, you had better find out before you get married (or give the impression of being married) how many days she spent in the UK in the previous 3 years, just in case you make a capital gain in due course.

They could have advised you to insist on a pre nuptial agreement which included a specific warranty regarding the days spent in the UK in the preceding 3 years.

(It might be thought that if they were not married in the earlier year then it should not matter because she would not have been a spouse in that earlier year and could not therefore represent a family tie at that time. Unfortunately not. The issue here is whether she was resident in the earlier years by reference to her own circumstances irrespective of her marital status at the time.)

10. Using a UK double tax treaty to work in the UK free of UK income tax

The general rule is that if you have a UK employment the earnings from that employment are subject to UK income tax. This applies irrespective of your residence status.

However, this is not the full story, as the terms of a UK double tax treaty will impact on this. In many cases this can be used to exempt any UK salary from UK income tax.

What does the double tax treaty say?

Paragraph (1) of the OECD Model Article sets out the general principle that salaries may be taxed in the country where the employment is carried out.

It follows from this that, in general, an individual can be taxed on the income arising from duties performed in the UK whether or not he is resident in the UK under our domestic law. This is in accordance with the UK's domestic provisions above.

However the tax treaties go one step further and provide that in certain circumstances the UK employment income can be exempted from UK tax.

Paragraph (2) of the OECD Model Article provides that, notwithstanding paragraph (1), employment income may, if certain conditions are fulfilled, be exempt from tax in the country where the employment is exercised.

Therefore this article forms the basis of most claims for exemption from UK tax for employees.

To qualify for exemption, the employee has to show that he is a resident of the other country for the purposes of the agreement. If therefore he could be classed as UK resident as well as resident abroad he would need to look at the tie breaker rules and ensure he was treaty resident abroad.

In addition there are a number of other conditions that would need to be satisfied:

In the UK for less than 183 days

The first condition for exemption is that the employee must not be present in the UK for more than 183 days either:

- `in the tax year concerned' or
- `in any period of 12 months'.

These two tests are completely different and are used in different treaties. The second test is more difficult to satisfy than the first one.

The agreements with: Azerbaijan, Belgium, Bolivia, Denmark, Estonia, France, Ghana, Guyana, Iceland, Indonesia, Ivory Coast, Kazakhstan, Korea, Latvia, Malta, Mexico, Mongolia, Norway Pakistan, Papua New Guinea, Sweden, Uganda, Ukraine, Uzbekistan, Venezuela and Vietnam use the wording of the second agreement (ie in any period of 12 months).

Most of the UK's other agreements use the other test.

For example, a US resident seconded to work in the UK for a two year assignment arrives here on 15 October 2021 and leaves the UK on 1 October 2021.

Depending on all the circumstances, he could be taxable in the UK only for the year 2022/2023.

For the years 2021/2022 and 2023/2024 he could meet the condition because in both periods he was not present in the UK for 183 days `in the tax year concerned'.

By contrast, a Norwegian resident working in the UK would be taxable here throughout the period 15 October 2021 to 1 October 21 under the test in the agreement with Norway.

Note that when assessing the 183day test any part of a day, day of arrival, day of departure, and all other days spent in should be included in the calculation as a day the person is present in UK.

Salary not paid by a UK employer

Another condition to obtain the exemption is that the salary must be paid by, or on behalf of, an employer who is not UK resident.

The fact that an individual remains an employee of an overseas company does not on its own satisfy the test. Not only must the employee remain an employee of the overseas company but the salary in respect of which the exemption is claimed must be paid by the overseas employer and not, for example, by a UK subsidiary company to whom the employee may have been seconded.

Salary not borne by permanent establishment in the UK

In a similar vein to the above the salary of the employee must not be borne by a permanent establishment or fixed base which the employer has in the UK.

This will need to be considered if an employee works in the UK for a non-resident company.

If the employee can meet these requirements they can claim an exemption from UK income tax on the UK salary earned.

The type of individual most likely to be affected by this is the foreign executive employed by a multinational group who is seconded to the UK.

If the UK secondment is relatively short the individual may still be regarded as resident in his home State under its tax laws while having acquired UK residence status under the domestic rules.

He'd therefore need to show treaty residence abroad as well as meeting the other conditions as above before he could then make a claim for exemption of employment income from UK tax in accordance with the tax treaty.

ABOUT THE AUTHOR

Lee Hadnum LLB ACA CTA is an international tax specialist. He is a Chartered Accountant and Chartered Tax Adviser and is the Editor of the popular tax planning website:

www.wealthprotectionreport.co.uk

Lee is also the author of a number of best selling tax planning books.

OTHER TAX GUIDES

Tax Planning Techniques Of The Rich & Famous - Essential reading for anyone who wants to use the same tax planning techniques as the most successful Entrepreneurs, large corporations and celebrities

The Worlds Best Tax Havens 2021/2022 – 220 page book looking at the worlds best offshore jurisdictions in detail

Non Resident & Offshore Tax Planning – Offshore tax planning for UK residents or anyone looking to purchase UK property or trade in the UK. A comprehensive guide.

Tax Planning With Offshore Companies & Trusts: The A-Z Guide - Detailed analysis of when and how you can use offshore companies and trusts to reduce your UK taxes

Tax Planning For Company Owners – How company owners can reduce income tax, corporation tax and NICs

Buy To Let Tax Planning – How property investors can reduce income tax, CGT and inheritance tax

Asset Protection Handbook – Looks at strategies to ringfence your assets in today's increasing litigious climate

Working Overseas Guide – Comprehensive analysis of how you can save tax when working overseas

Double Tax Treaty Planning 2021/2022 – How you can use double tax treaties to reduce UK taxes

Printed in Great Britain
by Amazon